# Business Visibility
# with Enterprise
# Resource Planning

# Business Visibility with Enterprise Resource Planning

Anupama Sakhare

PARTRIDGE
A Penguin Random House Company

**To order additional copies of this book, contact**
Partridge India
000 800 10062 62
orders.india@partridgepublishing.com

www.partridgepublishing.com/india

# Contents

## 5   Business Benefits of ERP                    37

# Appendix                                          51
# Job Opportunities in SAP                           51

# CHAPTER 1

# Introducing ERP

## 1.1 Introduction

In the past several years, Enterprise Resource Planning (ERP) systems have been successfully implemented by many Companies and Organizations. ERP systems are implemented using software packages such as SAP (Systemanlyse programment wicklung), Peoplesoft and Oracle.

The basic reason for implementing ERP system is to replace the numerous traditionally used Legacy Systems. This is also important for the utilization of Resources used in the Enterprise which deserve profitability but their potential is under - utilized and suppressed which does not allow the Organization to grow thereby affecting the stand of an organization and the business visibility in the global economic scenario.

There are a variety of business justifications and reasons for using ERP such as replacement of legacy systems, reduction in cycle times and reduction in operating costs in business.

## 1.2 What is ERP?

An ERP system is packaged business software system that allows a company to

1. Automate and integrate the majority of business processes.
2. Share common data and commonly used Business Practices across the enterprise .
3. Produces and access information in a real-time environment .
4. ERP supports multiple business functions and uses an "integrated systems" approach to provide business benefits.

## 1.3 Business Benefits of ERP ?

The ERP system is used to achieve the following business benefits:

1. All business processes require less time with ERP and the cost is reduced.
2. There is a faster transaction processing.
3. Financial Management is achieved using Modern Integrated Financial Management System with value added system and services, Moral Stand, Profit Center with sophistication offered by using Accounting Performance Measurement and automated Audit Trail.

4. The **"Best Business Practices"** are used and all existing Business Processes are re-engineered with a new Business Model.

5. Responsiveness to customers and suppliers helps to improve Productivity.

6. Linkage in established between suppliers and customers.

7. **e- Business** is implemented using improved Structural Transformation offered in organizations which is the cause of a revolution in the Best Business practices and Business Rules.

8. Cross – functional access to the same data and widely available information.

9. Facilitates organizational communications with customers and suppliers.

10. ERP provides reduced operating costs.

## 1.4 Business Needs and ERP :

From the Business point of view ERP fulfills the following needs of Business:

1. **Cycle Time:** Business Time and cost are reduced for all the business processes.

2. **Transaction Processing:** All the transactions are processed using the common data. ERP reduces the time and cost of multiple transaction updates.

3. **Financial management:** It requires very less amount of excess inventory and reduction in accounts receivable thereby improving operational performance.

4. **Business processes:** ERP offers the **"Best Rules"** for e-business and observes **" Best Business Practices"** by Re-engineering around a Standard Business Model.

5. **Productivity:** It helps to improve productivity by improving the financial management system by offering Profitable Business and better Value added Customer Service.

6. **Supply Chain Management:** The integration of ERP Modules supports the **"Integrated Systems"** approach by Linkages between suppliers and the customers.

7. **e - Business:** The Organization Structure observed in Legacy Systems is transformed into improved Structure which offers web-based interfaces which Support Integrated systems instead of isolated components.

8. **Information:** Widely available information is provided by ERP which is useful for Planning and Control of the same data which flows in the Organizational Resources thereby allowing **Cross-functional Access** to the same data.

9. **Communications:** Customers and suppliers are highly benefited by ERP because it facilitates Organizational Communications.

10. **Profitability:** Since there are common interfaces across the ERP Modules, the Profit aspect of Business is maximized using ERP.

## 1.5 Objectives of ERP

ERP system achieves a number of important objectives such as the following:

1. Maximizing throughput of information.
2. Maximizing Response Time to Customers and Suppliers.
3. Puts decision making down to the Lowest appropriate Level.
4. Provides timely information to decision makers.
5. There are various factors which hamper and hold back the Business Objectives such as Political interferences, high social overheads, business reluctant unions, multiplicity of controls etc. which are totally eliminated by the ERP system.

## 1.6 Performance Benefits of ERP

The following are the Benefits of ERP which strongly focus on the Business performance:

1. Information response time is fast.
2. There is an increased interaction across the enterprise.
3. Order management / Order Cycle time is improved.
4. Offers decreased Financial close cycle.
5. Improves interaction with customers.
6. Improves on- time delivery.
7. Improves interaction with suppliers

8. Operating costs are reduced.
9. Inventory Levels are lowered.
10. It offers Market Leadership.

## 1.7 Entries as inputs in ERP

A transaction of entry, checking and posting data can take place directly with the ERP Modules. A transaction can also direct data to other Business Applications within the ERP Framework.ERP follows the **Document Principle** which is used by the Controlling Unit in the ERP system which serves as an important evidence in the audit of each and every task element.

The design of an ERP Document includes Standard data entry functions which are in excess of the requirements of the Generally Accepted Accounting Principles (GAAP).

▪ **Types of Entries**

There are two types of entries:

1. Manual Invoice Entries
2. Recurring Entries

1. **Manual Invoices Entry :**
   One can enter, post a check received and match the payment to the specific open items in the customer accounts, all in one operation.

The successful posting of a transaction does not occur until the necessary data is recorded as an **ERP Document.**

The ERP system generated Document Header shows the date of posting, documents date, document reference number, and currency key.

The successful posting of a Business Transaction does not occur until the necessary data is recorded in the ERP System Document which is complete and error-free.

One can set aside a transaction document before is ready for posting, in which case the system will validate any information which has been entered and the system reports any discrepancies if traced in the transaction.

**Example:** The body of the document will contain one or more line items which will show the amount and identify the product and the terms of payment. The system will generate certain line items such as tax entries, cash discount, exchange rate difference as applicable.

2. **Recurring Entries :**
   A recurring entry is a set of data that will not be used until the due dates. Until then, the entries will not update account balances.

If the first date, the last date and the frequency or time interval between the entries is specified then the system will automatically post the required transaction on each of the due dates. As for example the monthly service fees.Instead of posting a series of entries one can set up a recurring entry.

- **Impetus for Business Process Change :**
  While still working in an independent environment or in an independent country or a product management organization, Business operations are blocked because the power still resides in the old functional Departments which provide a roadblock to rolling out the Standardized Business Processes.

  As the organizations implement ERP, they are moving away from the **"silos"**, or the specific units used by the Legacy Systems which are typically focused on products, regions or functions, to Standardized Business Operations used worldwide, by instituting common processes and by re-designing business processes and adopting the best business practices.

# Chapter 2

# Technology used in ERP

## 2.1 ERP Infrastructure

Enterprise Resource Planning makes use of the following technologies:

1. ERP software
2. Client – Server Environment
3. Integrated Databases
4. Business Intelligence using
   Data Warehouses
   Data Mart and
   Date Mining
5. ERP relies upon the use of Information Technology Infrastructure such as

   - Desktop – O/S Windows 98, NT, 2K and Apple 9, X
   - Server – O/S NT4 and 2K
   - Networking with the required Ports
   - Internet Access
   - Domain Name

- Backup Facility

ERP also relies essentially upon Client – Server Computing and Shared Databases.

The characteristics of Client – Server Computing include:

1. Increased Power
2. Increased Control
3. Increased Efficiency
4. Improved User Interfaces (GUI)
5. Improved Database Control.

## 2.2 ERP Architecture:

There are basically 2 components in the ERP Architecture.

(I) BASIS System Component
(II) ERP Applications Component

**System Component:** ERP System comprises a BASIS system to which application may be added.

The BASIS system provides a set of tools to build a suite of integrated programs that can be fitted exactly to the requirements of a Company which may be changed as the Company Develops.

Every ERP implementation needs a BASIS module that provides the elements of the runtime system. BASIS system is also called the Core system or the **Standard System.**

**ERP Applications Component:**

The ERP system operates by using the Client / Server principle applied across several levels.

The ERP system comprises a BASIS system to which application may be added.

Each application has several components which may be installed as required.

A component includes a range of functions which may be mandatory or optional.

## 2.3 ERP – BUSINESS MODULES

The following Business Modules are available in SAP Package. It offers an Integrated Standard Business Software for supporting major business functions.

The Integrated Standard Business Software Comprises of the following components or Business Modules.

1. CA - Cross Application
2. FI - Financial Accounting
3. CO - Controlling
4. IM - Capital Investment Management
5. EC - Enterprise Controlling
6. TR - Treasury
7. PS - Project System
8. LO - Logistics General
9. HR - Human Resources
10. PP - Production Planning

11. MM - Materials Management
12. PM - Plant Maintenance
13. QM – Quality Management
14. SD – Sales and Distribution
15. INT – International Development
16. IS – Industry Solutions

## 1. CA – CROSS APPLICATION MODULE:

The SAP R/3 Cross Application area comprises of a set of modules that can be used throughout the R/3 system.

- CA – BPT Business Process Technology
- CA – DM Document Management
- CA – CL Classification
- CA – CAD Integration

SAP R/3 Release 3.0 version includes cross application components which are available also in the earlier releases and additional integrative modules that are coded without the "CA" prefix.

- SAP Office
- SAP Business Workflow
- R/3 Business Engineering Workbench which includes the R/3 Reference Model and R/3 Implementation Model.
- R/3 Business Navigator, which includes the R/3 Process Model, the R/3 Data Model and the R/3 Customizing System
- R/3 Analyzer, is available online with the R/3 system or as a stand-alone PC- based system and it is used to access the R/3 Reference Model

In addition to these modules there are two more modules which are used in the context of cross-application. They are

- OSS – Online Service System
- CCMS – Computing Center Management System

## 2. FI – FINANCIAL ACCOUNTING MODULE:

The Financial Accounting Module comprises the following sub – systems:

- FI- GL General Ledger
- FI – AR Accounts Receivable
- FI - AP Accounts Payable
- FI - LC Legal Consolidation
- FI – SI Special Purpose Ledger

## 3. CONTROLLING MODULE :

The Controlling Module comprises the following sub – systems:

- CO – OM Overhead Cost Control
- CO – PC Product Cost Controlling
- CO – ABC Activity Based Costing
- CO - PA Sales and Profitability Analysis
- CO – PRO Project Control

## 4. IM – CAPITAL INVESTMENT MANAGEMENT:

- IM – FA Tangible Fixed Assets
- IM – FI Financial Investments

## 5. EC- ENTERPRISE CONTROLLING MODULE:

- EC- EIS Executive Information
- EC – BP Business Planning
- EC – MC Management Consolidation

- EC- PCA Profit Center Accounting

## 6. TR- TREASURY MODULE :
- TR- TM Treasury Management
- TR- FM Funds Management
- TR-CM Cash Management

## 7. QUALITY MANAGEMENT:
- QM - PT Planning Tools
- QM – IM Inspection Management
- QM – QC Quality Control
- QM –CA Quality Certificates
- QM – QN Quality Notifications

## 8. PS – PROJECT SYSTEM:
- PS – BD Basic Data
- PS – OS Operational Structures
- PS – PLN Project Planning
- PS – APP Project Approval
- PS – EXE Project Execution / Integration
- PS – IS Information System

## 9. LO- LOGISTICS GENERAL :
- LO – LIS Logistics Information System
- LO- MD Master Data
- LO- PR Forecast
- LO – VR Variant Configuration
- LO – ECH Engineering Change Management

## 10. HR – HUMAN RESOURCES:
The HR Human Resources application has been developed to provide an integrated human resource

management system by facilitating the use of the components of the –

1) PD- Personal Planning and Development module and the
2) PA – Personnel Administration Module. HR module comprises of the following modules.

- **HR–PD PERSONAL PLANNING AND DEVELOPMENT MODULE**
    - PD – OM Organizational Management
    - PD – SCM Seminar and Convention Management
    - PD – PD Personnel Development
    - PD – WFP Workforce Planning
    - PD – RPL Room Reservations Planning

- **HR – PA PERSONNEL ADMINISTRATION MODULE**
    - PA – EMP Employee Management
    - PA – BEN Benefits
    - PA – COM Compensation Administration
    - PA – APP Applicant Management
    - PA – TIM Time Management
    - PA – INW Incentive Wages
    - PA – TRV Travel Expenses
    - PA – PAY Payroll

## 11. PP – PRODUCTION PLANNING MODULE
- PP – BD Basic Data
- PP – SOP Sales and Operations Planning
- PP – MP Master Planning

- PP - CRP Capacity Requirements Planning
- PP – MRP Materials Requirements Planning
- PP- SFC Production Orders
- PP – PC Product Costing (which also is also called CO- PC Product Cost Accounting)
- PP - KAB Kanban / Just- in-Time Production
- PP - REM Repetitive Manufacturing
- PP – ATO Assembly Orders
- PP- PI Production Planning for Process Industries
- PP – PDC Plant Data Collection
- PP – IS Information System

## 12. MM – MATERIALS MANAGEMENT MODULE

- MM – MRP Material Requirements Planning
- MM - PUR Purchasing
- MM – IM Inventory Management
- MM – WM Warehouse Management
- MM- IV Invoice Verification
- MM –IS Information System
- MM – EDI Electronic Data Interchange

## 13. PM – PLANT MAINTENANCE MODULE

- PM - EQM Equipment and Technical Objects
- PM – PRM Preventive Maintenance
- PM – WOC Maintenance Order Management
- PM – PRO Maintenance Projects
- PM – SMA Service Management
- PM – IS Plant Maintenance Information system

## 14. SD – SALES AND DISTRIBUTION

- SD – MD Master Data
- SD - GF Basic Functions

- SD- SLS Sales
- SD- SHP Shipping
- SD – BIL Billing
- SD – CAS Sales Support
- SD – IS Information System
- SD –EDI Electronic Data Interchange

## 15. INT – INTERNATIONAL DEVELOPMENT MODULE
- IN – APA Asian and Pacific Area
- IN – EUR Europe
- IN – NAM North America
- IN – AFM Africa / Middle East
- IN – SAM South America

## 16. IS – INDUSTRY SOLUTIONS MODULE
This module comprises of ERP e-Business Solutions applied to a specific industry. The following are examples of Industry Solutions:
- IS – PS Public Sector
- IS – H Hospitals
- IS – B Banks
- IS – IS Real Estate Management

# 2.4 Business Process Re-engineering

The major motivations for business process re-engineering are

1. Customer sophistication using CRM
2. Deregulation and
3. Increasing competition on a global level.

- **Value Chain :**

In order to understand business process re-engineering, it is important to understand the concept of Value Chain. The Value Chain consists of two types of activities of the firms:

1. Primary Activities
2. Secondary Activities

I) The Value Chain : The Primary Activities of the firm include

   1. Business Functions
   2. Information Systems supporting all Primary Activities

II) The Value Chain : Secondary Activities include supporting business activities such as

   1. Organization (Electronic Mail)
   2. Human resources (Skills databases)
   3. Technology (CAD & CAM)
   4. Purchasing (with online links to various databases)

Re - engineering strives to attain the goal of efficient re-design of the Company's Value Chain. It focuses on the following important phases of the evolution and re-design of the Company in the context of Value Chain:

   1. Open Market Place
   2. Cooperation

3. Coordination at the Single – level and Multi – Level and

4. Full Collaboration

## 2.5 Elements of Business Re- engineering :-

The following are important elements of business re-engineering

1. Business Processes
2. Integration of Business Processes
3. Use of Technology
4. Cross- Functional coordination
5. Timing to improve processes

With the objective to implement market-driven strategies designed to provide a competitive edge.

The processes of Business process Re-engineering start with Process Modeling. The process Model comprise of:

1. **Business process**
2. **Data Store**
3. **Data Flow**
4. **The Organizational Unit**
5. **Events such as Triggers and other Outputs.**

**1. Business Process :**
The Business process reflects the business activities which need to be accomplished in a firm.

2. **The data store** :
   The data store consists of the data that are required by the business process.

3. **The data flow :**
   The flow directs the data which is being transmitted from one process to another process or between a process and a Data Store.

4. **The Organizational Unit**
   The organizational Unit depicts the units of organization in which these business processes take place (e. g. Accounts Payable, Payroll).

5. **Events** such as Trigger: A trigger is a procedure which is implicitly executed when an INSERT, UPDATE or DELETE statement is issued against the associated table.

   In addition, triggers are commonly used:
   - To automatically generate derived column values of the table.
   - To prevent invalid transactions.
   - Enforce complex Security authorizations.
   - Enforce referential integrity across nodes in a distributed database environment.
   - Enforce complex business rules
   - Provide Transparent Event Logging
   - Provide sophisticated auditing

- Maintain synchronous table replicates
- Gather statistics on table access

Any resistance at the country level / Manager Level is avoided by creation of Role to offer "Process Ownership".

# CHAPTER 3

# Business Re-design

## 3.1 Re-structuring Business Processes –

**The restructuring of Business Processes from Traditional Organization System to Re-engineered System is implemented on the basis of the following important factors :**

1. Job Design
2. Organization Structure
3. Career Moves
4. Work Rules
5. Management
6. Skills required

1. **Job Design:** In the Traditional Organization, job design is narrow, after re-engineering it become broad.
2. **Organization Structure:** It becomes Horizontal rather than Hierarchical as in the traditional systems.

3. **Career Moves:** Career move after re-engineering become horizontal rather than vertical as in the Traditional systems.
4. **Work Rules:** Work rules are judgmental from Business point of view rather than old Traditional Procedures.
5. **Management:** Re-engineered organization offers Market Leadership rather than only supervision of Business Activities.
6. **People skills required:** People skills are made Adaptive rather than Structured as in Traditional Organizations. It is important to consider the fact that all employees involved in the Business Process Management work must " buy into " the new Business Processes and understand and adapt their role in contributing to the success of the new system.

**Advantages of Re-engineering:**

ERP provides an opportunity to re-design business processes. The combination of a re-engineered job and information technology enables organizations to become:

1. More responsive to the changing markets.
2. Provide new opportunities such as e-Business.
3. Offers improved Productivity.
4. It reduces Costs.

## 3.2 Supply Chain Management

Through supply chain, customers and suppliers can partner with each other with the Business objective to maximize:

1. Responsiveness in Business and
2. Provide flexibility in Production

The objective of Supply Chain Management is to link all Business activities through the supply chain from the acquisition of raw materials to selling of the product to the customer. In the new supply chain, close partnerships exist between the manufacture and the retailer.

Transition from the old Supply Chain to the new Demand Chain shows the difference between old Supply Chain and New Demand Chain.

In the old supply chain, companies supplied customers with products using the Inventory system.

In the new demand chain companies use information about customer needs to manufacture products on the basis of customer's demand.

Supply chain Management is useful to forecast consumer's demand using the Shared Information available from the POS (Point-of-sale) transaction system to various Supply Chain partners such as:

1. Retailers
2. Distributors
3. Logistic units
4. Manufacturers and
5. Suppliers.

This shared information is useful for finding on-hand inventory, POS data by the Retailers; On-hand inventory, Retailers' orders, Shipping notices by the Distributors; In–transit inventory, planned shipments, Delivery Schedules by the Logistic Units; Material production schedule, Actual production Report, Distributors' orders, shipping notices by the Manufacturers.

The basic objective of Supply Chain Management is to respond to the customer's demand. All the entities involved in the process of Supply Chain Management such as Suppliers, Manufactures, Wholesaler and Retailer are subsequently benefited.

## 3.3 Cross – Docking:

Information about the customer's demand is generated through point-of-sale (POS) and it is transmitted every day.The customer purchase updates are used as sales forecasts and triggers are used to generate correct information regarding on-hand inventory and production schedules. Thus in the new system of Supply Chain Management the retailer's inventory can thus be maintained by the manufacturer. This innovative strategic system eliminates the cost involved in handing the product from the place of manufacture to the customer.

Cross-docking establishes linkages from customer to the supplier and eliminates the additional cost required for shipment of stock from the supplier to the retailer's distribution center. In cross-docking merchandise moves directly from inbound trucks to the outbound trucks, without getting stored in the Distribution and Inventory Block. This process maximizes profit and reduces costs.

## 3.4 Business Modules in an ERP Package:

The following business modules are used in an ERP package

1. Finance
2. Manufacturing
3. Human Resources
4. Plant Maintenance
5. Materials Management
6. Quality Management
7. Sales and Distribution

# CHAPTER 4

# ERP Modules

## 4.1. Financial Accounting Components

The basic objective of the Financial Accounting package is to

1. Increase revenues and
2. Reduce costs.

The module is used to perform Financial Accounting and Management Accounting functions.

Business decision making about product profitability is difficult when financial information is maintained in separate databases for different business functions such as marketing, production and purchasing.

Disintegrated database causes problems such as incorrect- data, missing data and inconsistent data. This causes a significant difficulty in the profitability measure and the overall business performance.

ERP helps to know and understand the causes underlying the following questions such as:

- Which products are most profitable?
- Which divisions are most profitable?
- Which customers are most profitable?

ERP supports the Financial Accounting module with the following subsystems

1. Credit Management
2. Product Profitability
3. Finished goods Inventory
4. Inaccurate Inventory Costing
5. Consolidating information from subsidiaries
6. Management Reports
7. Audit Trail Generation

Financial Accounting Module helps in maintaining the Quality of reports generated as expected by the general accounting standards as well as legal requirements.

At each step in the Information interconnection, the Document flow creates an Audit Trail to reflect documents such as

1. Order placed.
2. Order requirements transferred to Materials Management.
3. Picking requests as per transfer order.
4. Goods removed from Inventory for Packing.
5. Invoice and
6. Accounting entries posted.

The Key Financial management activities related to financial accounting includes:

1. Cost Center Accounting
2. Internal Orders
3. Activity- Based costing
4. Product Cost Controlling
5. Profitability Analysis
6. Profit Center Accounting
7. Consolidation of Financial data.

## 4.2 Interfacing of Financial Accounting module with other ERP Modules

The Financial Accounting Modules is linked with other ERP modules such as:

I. Materials Management:
   This is used for posting the cost of goods to Financial management Accounting

II. Production Planning:
   Posts the cost of bills of materials, which are created in production planning

III. Personnel Administration :
   This module posts expenses for payroll transactions.

IV. Sales and Distribution :
   This module posts revenue from billing documents.

- **Benefits of ERP**

    1. ERP Modules provide up-to-date information on cost variances, so that product pricing and profitability decisions can be made with accurate information.
    2. It creates a document flow for all business transactions.
    3. Helps in increasing Business Unit Performance Profitability.
    4. Reduces Costs.

## 4.3 Manufacturing Module

ERP Promotes Just-in-time (JIT) manufacturing thereby reducing the

    1. Response time
    2. Order Cycle time
    3. On-time delivery
    4. Low Inventory Level
    5. Flexibility in Production
    6. Decreased financial Close cycle

### ERP in a Manufacturing Enterprise:

ERP in a manufacturing enterprise seeks to achieve the following objectives:

    1. Greater product customization.
    2. Rapid introduction of new or modified products.
    3. Interactive customer relationships.

4.  Dynamic reconfiguration of production processes.

Greater product customization from manufacturing to order processing requires relatively very low unit cost.

New Virtual enterprise or Virtual Corporation combines together talents of the partner alliances to blend together "Core competencies" which yield new and modified products.

Customer relationship management is useful to innovate, entertain and enhance the product purchasing experience completely from product selection and ordering to receiving and service to best meet the needs and demand of customers.

Dynamic Reconfiguration of production processes would accommodate swift changes in product designs or bring about entire new product lines.

## 4.4 Motivation for manufacturing module:

Prior to ERP, the customers only dealt with distributors and retailers and the most important manufacturing unit was far removed from the customer. The disadvantage of removing manufacturing unit from the customer's demand caused-

1.  Excess Inventory
2.  Difference between costs-
    Standard costs and actual costs (such as Materials, Purchase, Production etc.)
3.  Customer's requirements and Customer Relationship Management (CRM) was ignored in business.

4. Inaccuracy, data inconsistency and Missing Data values led to Inaccurate Production Forecasts.

All this resulted in incorrect Business Decisions and Business Management.

The ERP Manufacturing Module is highly supported by using the Computer Aided Materials Requirement Planning (MRP).

## 4.5 ERP for Management Control includes:

1. Operational Data and
2. Activity – based cost (ABC) information used for Management Control.

   1. Operational Data includes data related to -
      Purchasing
      Receiving
      Quality Control
      Cost Accounting
      Materials Management
      Inventory Management

   2. Activity- based cost (ABC) - information which is used by the Manufacturing Module for Management Control includes-

      Material Requirement Planning (MRP)
      Just-in-time (JIT) Manufacturing
      Capacity Planning
      Production Scheduling

Product Design
- Computer Aided Design (CAD)
- Computer Aided Manufacture (CAM)

## 4.6 Computer Integrated Manufacturing

If too much products are manufactured then there is excess inventory which creates problems such as:-

1. Changing market needs are not considered
2. There is an imbalance of Demand and Supply
3. Cost is incurred in bulk storage and shipment
4. Right amount of quantity is not produced in time and
5. Excess Inventory creates problems.

The Computer-integrated Manufacturing System used in ERP is designed to integrate all Software and Hardware used in Manufacturing by integrating the entire Manufacturing databases.

## 4.7 Advantage of using Manufacturing Modules in ERP systems

1. These are fully integrated databases.
2. Paperwork is eliminated.
3. Design cost is decreased.
4. Lead time is decreased.
5. Productivity of Engineering and Design process is increased.
6. Work-in-process inventory is reduced.
7. Personnel costs are considerably reduced.

## 4.8 SAP Modules used in Production Planning

Each of the following modules provides important inputs to the subsequent module in the Production Planning process:

1. Sales and Operation Planning
2. Demand Management
3. Master Production Schedule(MPS)
4. Material Requirements Planning(MRP)
5. Manufacturing Execution
6. Order Settlement

# Chapter 5

# Business Benefits of ERP

## 5.1 Selection of ERP

These following steps are used in the ERP Selection process:

Step 1: Assessment of the Business.

Step 2: Appointment of a Selection team.

Step 3: Assessment of Business requirements and constraints.

Step 4: Determination of a selection criteria.

Step 5: To find Vendors.

Step 6: Communication with potential vendors.

Step 7: Shortlist and select ERP.

Step 8: Formalize the project plan ERP.

The primary goal of ERP system selection is to source a system that can provide functionality for all the business processes, which will get complete user acceptance and management approval.

## 5.2 SWOT Analysis

SWOT analysis for using ERP Products in Corporate Planning.

A variety of analytical tools and techniques are used in strategic planning. These tools include PEST analysis, Scenario Planning, Porter five forces analysis, SWOT analysis, Growth- share matrix, Balanced Scorecard and Strategy maps.

- **SWOT Analysis:**
  SWOT Analysis is used evaluate

  1. Strengths
  2. Weaknesses
  3. Opportunities and
  4. Threats

involved in a Project or in a Business venture.

A SWOT analysis can be carried out for a product, place, industry or person.

Strengths: Characteristics of the business or project that give it an advantage over others.

Weakness: Characteristics that place the business or project at a disadvantage relative to others.

Opportunities: Elements that the project could exploit to its advantage.

Threats: Elements in the environments that could cause trouble for the business or project.

## 5.3 Factors affecting SWOT Analysis

There are two types of key pieces of information for conducting SWOT analysis:

1. Internal Factors
2. External Factors

**Internal Factors:**
The Strengths and Weakness internal to the organization are evaluated using the SWOT analysis. Internal Factors may include the 4PS (Price, Product, Promotion and Place) as well as other internal factors such as Personnel, Finance, Manufacturing capability etc.

**External Factors:**
The Opportunities and threats presented by the environment external to the organization the external factors may include macroeconomic matters, technological change, legislation, socio-cultural changes as well as changes in the market-place or in competitive position.

## 5.4 Supply Chain enabled ERP

The POS(Point-of-sale) System is integrated with the Supplier link which creates Linkages between suppliers and retailers that translate into

1. Lower Costs
2. Better Customer Service
3. Supply of products on demand basis
4. Improved responsiveness and
5. Profitability for both partners

## 5.5 EDI

Inter-organizational Commerce is achieved using Electronic Data interchange (EDI).

EDI is aimed at forging boundary-less relationships in order to do business in a global marketplace.EDI is used in the light of highly competitive electronic commerce environment.

EDI is defined as the inter-process communication of business information in a Standardized Electronic form.

EDI Communicates business Information and other pertinent information related to business transactions between the computer systems of Companies, Government organization, small businesses and banks.

- **Benefits of EDI:**

1. Reduced paper- based systems.
2. Resolves inter business problems.
3. Provides improved Customer Relationship Management.
4. Offers expanded Customer/Supplier base.

## 5.6 "Best Business Practices"

ERP Systems basically work on the concept of using **"Best Business Practices"** in order to:

1. Avoid Legacy Systems
2. Simplify and Standardize system
3. Gain Strategic Advantage
4. Improve CRM and SCM
5. Upgrade Systems
6. Link to global activities
7. Restructure the Company Organization

If they are used in small company organizations especially in the non-manufacturing type of trading and traditional systems then many problems related to the business growth are likely to arise due to:

1. Lack of integration between production and planning
2. Lack of integration between sales and purchases
3. Lack of integration between financial management and the Financial Accounting which affects the business in terms of profitability.

Production planning and Manufacturing is essentially an important module to achieve the maximum and perfect benefit of Enterprise Resource Planning.

As for example consider only the HR-Module, if the HR module is not linked with the other modules an important resource such as the Human Resource will remain un-utilized or under-utilized in terms of Profitability in e-Business and International Commerce.

ERP systems are instrumental in integrating manufacturing processes and other business processes by adopting the "Best Rules" of business and by implementing the "Best Business Practices". This separates the traditional approach of doing business from e-Business.

The evolution of co-ordination eliminates the old organizations in terms of job design, structure, career moves, working rules, the management and people skills needed.

It does not promote organizational rivalry and any such hindrance in establishing interactive business relationships from open Market to full Collaboration through cooperation, single-level and multi-level co-ordination and in Collaboration linked across the supply chain.

## 5.7 Traditional Systems Development Life Cycle

Traditional Approach of systems design includes the following phases:

1. Problem Definition
2. Feasibility Study
3. System Analysis
4. System Design
5. Detailed Design

6. Implementation
7. Maintenance

**1. Problem Definition:**
In this phase the problems in the existing system are identified. The tools and techniques used are interviewing and data collection.

**2. Feasibility study:**
In this step assignment is made to find the economical, technical, behavioral and management feasibility. The tools and techniques used to study are preliminary cost analysis.

**3. Systems Analysis:**
In this phase a detailed analysis of the present system is done which would include all processes, information flows and work organization. Various logical models are used in the phase such as-

Process models, data models, Organization charts and Hierarchy diagrams are used to analyze the system.

**4. Systems Design:**
Developmental design of the complete system is done for the proposed system which includes logical process models and logical data models for the proposed system.

**5. Detailed Design:**
Input, Process and Output design is finalized and program design for the proposed system is completed. The tools and techniques include forms design, database

design, input-output specifications and the program design specifications are finalized.

### 6. Implementation:
This includes the software implementation using coding, testing and documentation. This phase also includes end-users training, development of reporting systems, design of controls and security.

### 7. Maintenance:
This phase includes ongoing technical support for training, upgrades and modifications in the system.

## 5.8 ERP Implementation Life Cycle

ERP Implementation Life Cycle includes the following phases:

1. Planning
2. Requirements Analysis
3. Design
4. Detailed Design
5. Implementation
6. Maintenance and Continuous improvement.

### 1. Planning:
In this phase a business need assignment is conducted based on the business needs of the existing and the proposed system, a business justification is done using interview technique and cost justification.

### 2. Requirements analysis:

Selection of an ERP system is done by using the best practices and modules to see what the company can gain by implementing the new system.

### 3. Design:
In the design phase business process re-engineering is applied by using the ERP methodology's best practices or customized version of the software.

### 4. Detailed design:
A detailed design is selected by using interactive prototyping and by choosing standard inputs, processes and outputs (For example customer lists, vendor lists)

### 5. Implementation:
In this phase of Configuration, data is migrated from the old system to the new system and interfaces are developed. There is an implementation in which the vendors correct the "bugs or errors" and then by using the clean processes and data and develop interfaces. Reporting tools are also used in this phase. Reporting systems, tests controls, and security is implemented and end-users are trained.

### 6. Maintenance phase:
In this phase of the ERP Life cycle technical support is provided to the staff and users. Upgrades and enhancements are added to the existing modules.

- **ERP Implementation Methodology:**
  ERP Implementation Methodology involves the following elements:

  1. Re- engineer existing Business processes.
  2. Integrate all Business processes.
  3. Use of Technology in Business.
  4. Cross- Functional Business Co-Ordination.
  5. Improved time and responsiveness to market needs.
  6. Fulfillment of Business objective to attain market leadership.

- **Organizational changes:**
  This methodology is offered by using job re-structuring by

  1. Making the Job design broad rather than narrow.
  2. Changing the structure of the organization from hierarchical to flat.
  3. By making career moves Horizontal from vertical.
  4. By making work rules judgmental from procedural.
  5. Changing the role of management to offer market leadership rather than only supervision.
  6. By changing people skills from structured to be in adaptive roles.

- **Responsibility of the Business Organization:**

  1. To make the ERP Methodology work, all employees in the organization must "buy

into" the new processes and understand their individual role in their contribution to the success of the re-engineered system.
2.  To strengthen Customer Relationship Management.
3.  To link the raw materials to retail customers by Supply Chain Management.
4.  To create e-Business Value Chain.

## 5.9 ERP Cost / Benefit Analysis

Most firms implement a single ERP Package rather than selecting different modules from different ERP vendors.

However following Implementation Approaches may be used:

1.  Single ERP package with all required modules.
2.  Single ERP package used in combination with other systems.
3.  Multiple ERP packages used with other systems.
4.  Partial ERP Implementation.
5.  Totally in-house ERP system.
6.  In- house ERP with other specialized packages.

Each of these systems have their own price and their own costs and benefits based on various factors such as data integration, cost-effectiveness, competitiveness, business impact and time consumed. Most organizations prefer a single ERP package implementation to in-house development or maintaining the traditional legacy system.

## 5.10 Tangible and Intangible Benefits of ERP

Tangible Benefits of ERP include:

1. Inventory Reduction.
2. Personnel Reduction.
3. Productivity Improvement.
4. Order Management Improvement.
5. Financial Close cycle reduction.
6. Information Technology cost reduction.
7. Procurement cost reduction.
8. Cash management improvement.
9. Revenue/ Profit increase.
10. Transportation / Logistics cost reduction.
11. Maintenance reduction.
12. On-Line delivery improvement.
13. Provides Business Intelligence.

Intangible Benefits include:

1. Information/ Business Visibility.
2. New / Improved Business Processes.
3. Customer Responsiveness.
4. Integration of Databases.
5. Standardizations of Procedures and Documents.
6. Flexibility in Production.
7. Globalization of Business.
8. Business performance.
9. System up-gradation.
10. Creates Value chain in the Virtual Corporation.

## 5.11 ERP Vendors

The major ERP Vendors, include SAP, Oracle and PeopleSoft .The following business functions are supported by these vendors.

| Function | SAP | Oracle | PeopleSoft |
|---|---|---|---|
| Sales Order Processing | Sales and Distribution Module **(SD)** | Marketing Sales Supply Chain | Supply Chain Management |
| Purchasing | Materials Management Module **(MM)** | Procurement | Supplier Relationship Management |
| Production Planning | Production Planning Module **(PP)** | Manufacturing | |
| Financial Accounting | Financial Accounting Module **(FA)** | Financials | Financial Management Systems |
| Management Accounting | Controlling **(CO)** | | |
| Human Resources | Human Resources **(HR)** | Human Resources | Human Capital Management |

Source: Vendor websites

**Table: ERP Modules Supported by vendors**

Vendors addressing the mid-cap market ($50-$400 range) include Microsoft's Great Plains ERP Software.

The most common approach is to use a single ERP Package .

## 5.12 Causes of ERP Project Failures

Causes of ERP Project Failures include:

1. Resource failures
2. Requirement failures
3. Goal failures
4. Technique failures
5. User contact failures
6. Organizational failures
7. Technology failures
8. Size failures
9. People Management failures
10. Methodology failures
11. Planning & Control failures
12. Personality failures

# Job Opportunities in SAP

These are real-life examples of job descriptions prepared by recruitment companies which are presented here.

SAP –Related job descriptions are grouped as follows:

   I.   **Description of jobs carried out in SAP Subsidiaries.**
   II.  **SAP- Related job Description Advertised on the Internet.**
   III. **Jobs with SAP Business Partners**
   IV.  **Job Description of jobs with End–Users**

## I) Description of jobs carried out in SAP Subsidiaries

The structure of jobs available in SAP subsidiaries and SAP partners is changing and it differs according to the history of the company and the work areas which it provides. Some of the Job titles along with its scope are listed as follows:

1. **Account Executive (Customer Support Manager)**
2. **Alliance Partner Manager**
3. **Business Consultant**
4. **Industry Manager (Sales)**
5. **Instructor**
6. **Product Manager**
7. **Remote Consultant**
8. **Senior Consultant**
9. **Senior Remote Consultant**

1. **Account Executive (Customer Support Manager) Job Responsibility:**

   - Responsible for the measurement of Customers Satisfaction by being the principal point of contact throughout the time that the organization remains a customer.
   - Understands customers needs and to apply SAP solutions to meet these needs.
   - Maintain multiple customer relationships simultaneously within one or more vertical market sectors.

   **Experience:**

   - Experience of implementing enterprise-wide software solutions.

- Fundamental understanding of Business issues.
- Track record of empathizing with customer to achieve results and management of long-term customer relationship.

**Functional knowledge:**

- An expert in relationship building.
- Provide logical methodology to servicing a customer's requirements.
- Liaisons between partners and SAP to ensure customers satisfaction.
- Monitors customer satisfaction on a regular basis.
  And also has the following attributes -
- Product knowledge
- Industry knowledge
- Technological knowledge or Business vertical
- Assignment Management
- Leadership / Teamwork
- Communication Ability
- Act as a Trainer
- Business Development

2. **Alliance Partner Manager**: Leads, develops and manages partner relationships to ensure company and customer satisfaction and to generate revenue targets.

3. **Business Consultant**: The job scope presents a business focused SAP Solution to Prospective customers by using in-depth knowledge of one or more vertical markets, and is instrumental within the industry team in facilitating the sale.

4. **SAP Consultant**: Leads consulting assignments to support customers in the implementation of a SAP solution to satisfy a Business need.

5. **Industry Manager (Sales)**: The job Scope of Industry Manager (Sales) relates to the achievement of the sales and support revenue target for the industry sector and to achieve customer satisfaction and reference ability by working as a team player.

6. **Instructor**: Instructor is responsible for maintaining the quality of training systems and documentation and for giving courses in one or more application areas.

7. **Product Manager:** Develops a single point of contact for all issues related to a specific area of the product suite and offers complex assignments to support customers in the implementation of a SAP solution to satisfy a business need.

8. **Remote Consultant:** Provides first–line applications support to customers in specified application areas.

9. **Senior Consultant:** Leads multiple and /or complex assignments to support customers in the implementation of a SAP solution to satisfy a business need.

10. **Senior Remote Consultant:** Provides first–line applications support to customers in specified application areas.

## II) SAP – Related Job Description advertised on the Internet:

1. SAP Development Team.
2. SAP R/3 Installation Tools Developer.
3. Senior SAP R/3 Software Developer to enhance the Error Tolerance of SAP's R/3 BASIS Software.
4. SAP R/3 Software Developer.
5. ISS Internal Service Systems.
6. Software Developers: HR – Human Resource Systems International Developments.
7. Software Developers: HR-Human Resource Systems Personnel Administration and Payroll.
8. Product Developers: Patient Management/ Accounting (IS-H) Module.
9. Software Developer: SAP R/3 IS-Oil.
10. Development of SAP R/3 : IS-Oil
11. Developer SAP R/3 Retail.
12. Documentation Developer.
13. Documentation Developer-Banking Sector.
14. Logo Partners.
15. SAP Consultant with "Big Six" Management Consultancy.

## III) Jobs with SAP Business Partners:

### 1. SAP R/3 Business Consultant:
The Business Consultant must be capable of presenting and demonstrating both the specific implementation philosophy and SAP R/3 functionality.

### 2. Implementation Partner
### 3. Application Engineers
### 4. Module Configurers for International Projects

## IV) Job Description of Jobs with End-Users:

The following first four positions do not require previous SAP Experience.

1. **Commercial Analyst**
2. **Financial Analyst**
3. **Systems Analyst**
4. **Project Leader**
5. **SAP Business Analyst**
6. **SAP Analyst**
7. **MIS Manager**

# About the Text

This text can be used at the undergraduate or graduate level for a course in ERP.

This text is designed to provide fundamental concepts on the plan, design and implementation of ERP systems. It can be used subsequently with other text on Advanced Modules of ERP Packages.

This book provides Basic Understanding of:
- ERP Concepts
- ERP Technology
- Business Re-design Process
- ERP Modules
- Business Benefits of ERP